MW00412126

People Pleasing Almost Killed Me

How I Broke Free Of This Silent Killer....

And You Can, Too

Carrie Campbell

ISBN: 978-1519691897

CARRIE CAMPBELL

To My Daughter Miyah...

I dedicate the words that flood these pages to you because, from the moment you were able to give to others, you started to do just that.

A heart as big as this entire planet that we inhabit, you would heal the world if you could, and all at the tender age of ten.

You give of yourself freely and without expectation of return from anyone. Your little heart has already felt the pains of hurt from walking in the footsteps of people pleaser.

It is my mission to ensure that your life is led always with self-love, in action, not merely in words.

For if you can harness the care for yourself first, your legacy will far exceed mine with all that you are, all that you can be, and all that you will create.

I love you.

৵৵৵

To My Husband Brian...

Who found understanding for the tears even though he couldn't relate.

Who stood patiently as I navigated the journey.

Who rode the pendulum as it swung to and fro.

Who gave me a reason to want to love myself first and face some of the darkest days of my life.

Let's build dreams together, achieve them, and create more.

Level it up... always.

CONTENTS

Foreword

What you will find in this book is nothing short of FREEDOM.

Let's face it, I could end it there, because that promise in and of itself is no small task, especially when it comes to giving this gift of freedom to the group of women across the globe that are the hardest to accept it (aka... the moms of the world).

Keep in mind, this promise is also coming from someone -- yours truly -- who only believes in only showing up by "always under promise, always over deliver" and is committed to Locking Down the TRUTH.

So there you have it, my dear friend and fellow mom. The question is, will you give yourself permission to accept MORE FREEDOM into your life?

This is most likely the exact reason why you find yourself here, holding this very book, seeking something more.

This FREEDOM can only begin by releasing yourself from the bullshit that's been binding via the thoughts, belief systems, and stories you were told were true from the time you were a little girl. At one point you grew out of believing that monsters lived under the bed and in the closet, which now seems quite silly, right?

What if you are living right now in a system of conformity that is just as silly as believing monsters are under the bed?

Are you ready for a new reality that doesn't include these lies that have only been limiting you and your life?

Enter stage right to this play you call your life, which you are directing, is The Mindset Master Coach & The Iconic Mom Mentor Carrie Campbell, whose presence you've called into your life and is why this very book is in your hands.

See, this gift of freedom she shares isn't by telling you how to do MORE & be MORE so your "Super Cape" can flow even more brightly in the wind for all to see. This would only play into the same bullshit that you've always been told and that, my friend, is exactly why you are seeking FREEDOM in the first place.

Carrie Campbell is that light and beacon shining the light on the freedom that is within your grasp, right in front of you, that you just can't see.

Right now you are standing facing your shadow, only seeing the dark, and wearing glasses that are simply keeping you in a fog. I urge you for yourself, your life, those that are waiting for you to show up TRULY in the gift that is you, and this includes your children, to start the journey.

What if it simply took reaching up to take off those foggy glasses creating an unclear view and simply turning towards the light? Your light. This light that is already inside you and has always been available to you.

As a single mother of two, I can completely relate to the journey we as moms find ourselves on, with a pull between worlds of being a mom, trying to find, honor, express, and have our own identity, mixed in with all the stories and perceptions society has told us it has to look like. I urge you to look around at the results we have from living in these stories and ask yourself if that is really the life experience you want?

I can tell you from my personal experience that as a mom striving to wear the "super mom" cape to show up as the "perfect mom" to the world usually left me on edge, unfulfilled, and experiencing a personality trait I like to call "bitch mom."

This wasn't the mom that I wanted to be. My true intention was to be fully connected, loving, and growing with my amazing little growth partners. On top of this, living according to these stories left me feeling completely disconnected from myself, my gifts, my abilities, internally broken and unfulfilled. This is the price we choose to pay when we buy into the bullshit of conformity.

Let's ask ourselves instead the right question here:

What really matters?

What the world sees or what your true life experience is with the precious little -- or big and growing -- growth partners we call our children?

My life shifted when I chose that my life experience is what mattered. It is because of that choice, giving myself permission to be happy and starting my own journey, that I now live in a completely different life experience. My daily norm is awesomeness in every area of my life and we all have the opportunity to make the same choice for ourselves.

How do you NOW create it? When you LOOK for evidence of what you are seeking, you find it. The moment you get just a taste of this amazing woman who is THE Iconic Mom, you will only want to know how to experience more of this joy, freedom, abundance, love and light.

Carrie Campbell is a gift in my life whom I absolutely adore, and I've seen her be that beacon for countless women across the globe. I'm honored that she asked me to write this foreword to her book and to hopefully inspire you to know what is really at hand for you if you simply choose to opt in.

Her message and guidance are heartfelt,

authentic, raw, and brilliant to guide you to the balance between being a mom, honoring who you are, and creating an amazing fulfilled life. No cape necessary. I'm excited for all of you starting this book to take off the cape and allow yourself the FREEDOM of being the BEST version of yourself.

—Marci Lock

The Body-Mind Mentor

The Silent Killer of People Pleasing

There I sat, paralyzed. The only light that filled the room was that which shone off my computer screen. The same screen that I had been staring at for what felt like hours.

Paralyzed in a sudden realization, one that to this day I still can't trace back to a particular moment in time. It was more a series of collective ones that led to the shocking reality of what was staring me straight in the face.

Tears at this point had already dried on my cheeks, leaving that feeling of crystallized salt stains I had grown to know all to well over the last several years.

The sobbing had stopped because I came to know it wasn't going to get me anywhere anyway. The pity party was done and all I was left with was my own reality.

Isn't that all that we are each ever left with?

Our own reality.

The reality that we created.

Sure, we create it collectively with those in our lives, but at the core it was ours to create in the first place.

So there I sat in my very first true vulnerable moment of awareness.

That raw cutting awareness that stings because you know that you have been hiding behind the veil of its cloak for a very long time.

You realize that every victimized thought and feeling you have ever had no longer holds up, because the knowledge that you played a hand in that victimized state slaps you square across the face.

"Carrie, you haven't been living, you have only been surviving (and just barely)." This cut through the thoughts that had been perseverating and raw emotions that had been suffocating me that evening.

It was 2009, the eve before my thirtieth birthday, and it was the night that changed my life.

Some would think that a year prior, when I decided to make the difficult decision to leave my marriage, would have been the life-altering moment that would define the rest of my life.

And yet the stark clarity that I had during that space in time, that night with nothing but the company of my computer screen, is what released me from the grip of the very thing that was holding me back.

Hi, my name is Carrie and I am a recovering people pleaser. People pleasing almost killed me and took my life.

As I type out those words now, I realize the almost laughable irony in that statement.

It may seem strange to equate people pleasing to the road of a drug user or alcoholic, but it was nothing short of the same.

An addiction.

A drug.

An obsession.

Something that controlled my actions and behaviors and led me down self-destructive paths that caused me and my loved ones pain.

I was breathless, and not in a good way, at the sudden epiphany that the cape I toted around my entire life was nothing more than the equivalent of a ball and chain weighing me down.

Countless years spent trumpeting myself internally at all my selfless acts toward humankind that were met with rationalizations of this nature:

"He needed me."

"Who else would she turn to?"

"I have to fix this, I am the only one who can."

"But if I am a good person, I will do this for him, her, them...."

I know you because I was you.

As you read this, you are nodding your head in acknowledgement of your own reality.

Perhaps your own salt stains forming at the base of your jaw before the teardrops hit the keyboard.

As you sit there relating to me and my story, I am going to ask you to stop and ponder this:

Are you prepared to let go of those traces of victimization that, like a spider clinging to his web in the wind you are holding strong to?

Are you prepared to stand up from the nestled confines that are keeping you safe right this very moment and go stare straight in your mirror at the reflection waiting?

A reflection that has waited for years for you to stop and care.

Not for others.

Not for him or her or they.

But for you.

To care enough about the only being who will be with you in the end of your days.

As a recovering people pleaser, I know what that quiet voice in your head is speaking to you right now in hushed tones.

It is laced with resentment for all the people who have not "seen" what you have done for them.

It is spewing out defense tactics in preparation for how you are finally going to make them see.

That voice -- your voice -- is ready to blow.

At the boiling point every people pleaser reaches where, when push comes to shove, you lash out with venom at the people around you or you retreat further into your shell, begging for the day that it all changes.

Yes, I know you well because that dance that felt like a waltz when you started so many years ago has become a dance of death. A dance that, with no partner, has left you spinning in circles trying desperately to end the tango.

People pleasing almost killed me. A slow suicide that left an empty void in my life.

I would stare at the reflection in the mirror, wanting to spit sour words of anger and fury at those who had taken advantage of me.

I blamed, I victimized, and I spiraled in it for years.

Until one night.

The eve of my most lucid awakening...

To give is not bad, but to not give to oneself is death.

As the clock neared midnight and the anniversary of my birth and my next decade were ticking closer, I found myself feeling like a child holding on tightly to the last traces of a security blanket, because it was all I knew.

Afraid to step forward into a world where I took care of myself and actually articulated the word "no" to people was the equivalent of base jumping.

Not that I have ever based jumped, but it is the closest I can come to finding the appropriate description.

Head first off a cliff into the vastness that holds a feeling I had only ever imagined. Fear coursing through my body at the knowledge I had no idea how to do any of this.

Then, as quickly as the fear struck, an overwhelming energy of possibility rushed in and I thought "This is what freedom feels like?"

And so I jumped.

Alone, throwing caution to the wind with a silent vow to myself that unearthed deep emotions of knowing, SURVIVING wasn't good enough anymore.

As the fluorescent lights on the stove top flipped to 12:00 a.m., I shut the top of my computer screen, stood up on shaky legs after that massive cathartic release, and went to bed.

Pulling the white down-filled comforter up close to my face and sinking into the warmth, I breathed for what felt like the first time in my life.

My eyelids, heavy with traces of lingering emotion, closed and my last thought floated through my mind's eye:

"Tomorrow I start living again."

As I near the end of this chapter, it is my hope you realize I have opened the door for you.

Connected to part of your soul that has been screaming at you through muffled or loud cries.

My story doesn't start and stop at this moment in time, and through the rest of this book I intend to let you walk through the door into my world.

Travel the path I travelled and feel it for every emotion that it is and was.

Our collective journeys are always far more similar than they are different; by the time you have turned the last page of this book, I have one simple request of you.

Make tomorrow the first day you start living again.

*** Start Living Now ***

Pause for a moment and feel this chapter. Don't feel it for my journey but for yours and answer these questions.

~ What are you feeling?

~ What eye opening thoughts did you have?

~ What are you feeling afraid of?

"In releasing from our greatest fears we find our greatest freedoms"

www.TheIconicMom.com

Go to The Iconic Mom and get access to more information, resources, tools and free downloads today.

Start Living The Way You Would Tell Your Kids To...

The Pain of People Pleasing

The oddity of this chapter is that even I, all these years later, find myself astounded by the reality that people pleasing actually caused me pain.

Not just the non-physical pain of a life lived with complete disregard of oneself, but the actual physical pain that came along with the experience.

There I sat curled into a ball. Cornered in between two cabinets in my kitchen, I rocked slowly back and forth in a fetal position.

Arms braced so tightly around my legs and pulled in tight to my chest that the color was starting to fade to a dull, lacklustre ashen tone as the blood drained from them slowly.

That nook had been my home that day for what felt like an eternity. I sat there softly murmuring to myself through periodic outbursts of tears.

They had started to form already on my arms: Dull white marks that raised into scarlet lines traversing the length of each of my upper arms from where, minutes ago, my nails clawed desperately at my alabaster skin, trying to find some sort of relief from what I was experiencing.

Embarrassment settled into me.

Shame coursed through me.

Fear ever present, as I knew he was at some point going to enter the apartment and find me there.

I had no expectation of Brian understanding what I was going through because, truth be told, I didn't have even an iota of clarity some 5 years ago as I rocked back and forth.

Over the last half decade, as I continue on this journey of life, I have come to understand the triggers that brought me to that point and gratefully learned how to ensure I never went back there.

If you are reading this and you are not a people pleaser or have yet to admit it, you might find yourself unable to relate or even understand how such gravity of a situation can be even remotely connected to something so, well, benign.

And yet, if you are one of the people pleasers reading this book who have become fully aware of how this cape of pride isn't so much that at all, you not only can understand this but you can relate to how all these dots connect.

I heard his footsteps ascending the front stairwell, inching closer to the door. Calling my name as he made his way through the threshold: "Smalls?" he said, trying to locate where I was in our quaint home that usually was the nest of security for me.

I nestled my head deeper into my arms and simply breathed. He turned the corner and let out an audible gasp.

The shame deepened as I knew it would take but a few seconds for his eyes to gaze upon the streams of red painting my arms.

His step softened, which for a 6 foot 3 man isn't hard to note. I could sense that he had crouched down in front of me before he softly whispered in that deep throaty voice of his I had come to love, "Carrie, look at me."

In that moment, I wanted to flee. I wanted to be anywhere but there.

The elephant on my chest wasn't just sitting anymore; he was jumping up and down with a pair of rock climbing spikes on.

In short, it hurt.

He was about to pose the dreaded question, "What's wrong?" I knew it, and my panic was simply that I had no idea.

How do you try to tell someone what is wrong when you have no clue what is going on yourself?

I was at the peak of angry but I wasn't an angry person.

I was pissed off at the world but that isn't in my nature.

I was sad and lonely but filled with happiness and joy.

The duality of it all was a little complex and a lot confusing.

I was consciously aware of what I was experiencing and yet totally unconsciously aware of what had triggered such a tornado of fury.

That day was by far, without question, one of the worst days of my 36 years on this planet.

Isolation soared through me as Brian pulled me into his arms, the safest place on Earth for me, which only created more strain. Strain because, in his hold, I realized I felt nothing that day.

The tremble that had found its place in my body was building to a furious shake; he pulled me close and just held on.

As I type this, I find myself wondering how we made it through that day. How I found the clarity that I did about what brought me to that state?

Today I find gratitude for that moment, as it was simply another bump on the journey of climbing the ladder to greater freedom.

So we sat there and waited. For the tears to stop flowing, the shaking to settle, and the pain in my heart to ease.

When I finally regained enough desire to move again, I stood in front of a mirror staring at myself.

My face swollen and puffy from the anguished tears that had fallen and my arms visibly standing out with the angry lines that had started to slowly fade.

I stood transfixed on those lines for a long time that night, vowing to find clarity after this moment so that I never had to walk in those shoes again.

As those scratches dissolved over the next few days, my mind grew more alert. The fog of emotion started to lift and I was able to start piecing together the puzzle that was seemingly missing all the pieces.

Yes, people pleasing brought me to that point, and I view it as my devotion to help you understand how, no matter how intricate a web it was, so that you never have to experience a moment such as I did, if you haven't already.

In moments of pondering the following week, I realized I could easily blame the "worst day of my life" on hormones, the stressors of my life, or the fact that I had been sick the few days prior.

I heard a voice in my own head snarl at me as if to say, "Are you really going to keep telling yourself that, Carrie?" because I knew that there was more to the story.

How did I come to undercover the truth, you ask?

I listened.

Not to others but to myself.

Lying in bed at night, I would stare out the window to the tree that poised itself outside our home, illuminated by the moon, and I would listen.

Sitting at my desk during the day in quiet moments in the back of my mind, I would listen.

Instead of doing and talking and concluding, I merely sat and listened to my thoughts that would surface, and I found my answers.

I came to realize that what happened on that dark day was merely a product of all the actions and behaviors I had allowed myself to take leading up to that moment.

The stories in my head were laced with hurt, filled with resentment, and victimized in the nature of their content.

The undercurrents of "He did this to me" or "How could she do that after I did this?" or "No one ever gives to me" were prominent in thought.

As I peeled back the layers of that oversized onion, however, I came to the shocking awareness that it wasn't "them," it was "me."

I had built a world of my own hurt by allowing it. Always doing for others and never doing for myself. Not speaking up and telling people when something didn't feel okay with me.

I had completely enabled a world where people took what I had to give but were conditioned by the permission I gave them to not give in return.

That led to years of suppression.

What had started out as hurt and sadness in given experiences developed into bitterness and anger at the people who had been so "inconsiderate" of me.

Now, don't think that I am sitting here condoning behaviors from others that are hurtful, far from it. We should all treat each other in kindness. But think about this: If you don't let others know you have been hurt, how can they possibly, even remotely understand and help create change?

If one doesn't know, there is absolutely nothing one can do.

As you read this, I suspect you are almost laughing at the completely obvious statement I just made. Yet all people pleasers do this, on both large and small scales.

It was the repeated years of suppression that led to that moment for me. The sadness, the loneliness, the anger that had been driven inward for so many years by none other than me finally started to come full circle.

Like a boiling pot with the lid on, it had been in a slow rumble for awhile. Ponder that pot for a second, the one you can hear from the other room. It is a soft clattering along the edges coupled with a few hissing noises as water hits the hot stove top.

What do you do?

You drop everything and go to the kitchen to turn it down, remove the lid, or take it off the heat, right?

With your life, however, you take a gamble. You let the pot sit on the heat swelling into a fury that is going to blow at a random moment in time when you are a few feet away.

I tiptoed out of the room, leaving Brian behind as he had already drifted off into a slumber a few nights after "the event." I went to our living room, which was lit dimly by the amber glow of a single light, and I started to put it all onto paper, much as I have asked you to do while reading this book.

All the realizations of every single moment that I could call upon that had been suppressed.

As the list grew, I realized that my pot had been boiling for a very long time.

What followed next was a duality of something I hope I can do justice to with words.

Terrifying fear clawed at me, telling me that if I kept letting my pot boil by holding things in,

I would one day find myself in a much worse scenario than that fetal position on my kitchen floor.

Yet I was paralyzed by this numbing fear at the same time, causing me to wonder if I could navigate around this pattern of behavior that I had known for so long.

Then I recalled the promise I made to myself several years prior: "I will live, no longer merely survive."

Knowing fully that in order for me to stay true to that commitment to myself, I had to find a way.

The next day, putting one foot in front of the other, both literally and metaphorically, I made my way to Brian to share what I had come to realize.

Accepting the fact that I had no one to blame for my state of being other than myself and choosing not to blame but to understand.

When you accept, you can take accountability, and from that you can create change.

Thankfully, those lines down my arms have faded, leaving nothing other than traces of a memory, not even a scar. A memory, however, that I plan to hold onto so that I never sit in that position again.

** Start Living Now **

Pause for a moment and feel this chapter. Don't feel it for my journey but for yours and answer these questions.

~ What situations do you currently have in your life that rather than changing you are merely suppressing?

~ When that situation reaches a boiling point what reactions do you experience?

~ Do you really think that reaction is normal?

"Suppression Offers You Nothing Other Than Something You Have To Deal With At A Later Date"

www.TheIconicMom.com

Go to The Iconic Mom and get access to more information, resources, tools, and free downloads today.

Start Living The Way You Would Tell Your Kids To

The 20-Foot Wall

Have you ever experienced a physical limitation where one did not exist?

The confusing feeling of a barrier surrounding you that, while you realize it is merely a perception, literally feels like a tangible reality between you and the rest of your life.

Sometimes so real in its strength that you feel like, if you were to reach your hand out, the force of what you are feeling internally would be felt to the naked touch of your fingertips?

That is what I felt most often during the early stages of my journey as a recovering people pleaser. The stark clarity of how I allowed this behavior to cripple my life had come and gone. The overwhelming feelings of sadness upon realizing that I had partially been responsible for sucking all the joy out of my life.

Something happens when you become aware and truly accept the path that was traveled of your own volition.

In a breathless, terrifying moment of panic, you realize that you have to do something with the awareness.

That no magic pill is available at the drugstore to heal this reality.

That there is no mystical wand that a fairy godmother will come and wave, giving you a "do over" in your life.

No, not in this reality.

While during the years as an active people pleaser I tolerated moments of sadness, frustration, bitterness and resentment, nothing compared to what I felt the day I came to realize, "I have to do something about this."

Isolation set in, coupled with an intolerable fear that was precipitated by questions such as:

"How do I fix this?"

"What if I can't?"

"What if, in the process I mess things up even more?"

Questions that had no answers to follow because there were none.

All I had in that moment of full accountability to take action and change my path was awareness and the decision to place one of my size seven feet in front of the other and start moving.

And so I did.

By now I suspect you have come to your own realizations of your people pleasing patterns, if they exist. You are likely able to identify times when you know that you are in the process of doing all the pleasing.

That is where I started because that was all I had, the knowledge of what had gotten me into this proverbial mess in the first place.

Rationally, it is a rather simple "fix" to implement: simply speak my mind and my thoughts in the moment.

Easy, right?

Wrong!

Dead wrong, as a matter of fact, and for many reasons. Indifference being one, but I will get to that a little later on.

For the purpose of this chapter, let me continue with the story of that wall.

So there I stood at the entrance of our grocery store, frozen in time.

I remember that moment so well and, as I type this, I chuckle out loud, only to have Brian ask me, "What are you laughing at?"

What am I laughing at? The ridiculous nature of this story as I look back all these years later and realize how deep my people pleasing tendencies ran.

I digress.

It was the evening rush and people were racing in and out of the store picking up their nightly needs.

The fast pace was notable because I stood paralyzed. Little 5 foot1 me staring up at all 6 foot3 of Brian with what I can only imagine looked to be the face of a young child getting caught with her hand in a cookie jar.

My bottom lip started to tremble as he asked me his question again.

The racing of my heart was threatening tears to spill over from my eyes, and I was utterly confused.

Mostly because, while I was able to recognize how simple the question he had asked me was, I was confused by the reality that, for some reason, between me and my answer was this impenetrable wall that was disallowing me to speak.

After you read this next part, I beg of you to stop and reflect on this. The simplicity of a question and the turmoil of an answer. For the record, I know factually that I am not the only one who has sat in this bracket of people pleasing. I have shared this story many times and always get resounding nods of acknowledgment that others "get it."

"What do you want for dinner? Chicken or steak? And before you tell me to pick, I am not picking. Tonight is your call."

The words reverberated through me as the panic that I had yet to understand set in.

At this point, Brian was aware of my people pleasing deficits and was simply trying to promote forward movement.

However, anytime a question was followed up with "I am not picking," the walls started to close in around me.

Isolated and alone.

I sat on the other side of what I can only define as a 20 foot brick wall. I was well aware that on the other side was freedom and that all I had to do was climb over it to get there, but the feat was impossible.

Not only did the walls feel tangible and real but the notion that they were closing in on me was also suffocating me.

The word "chicken" sat in my thoughts as I stared up at Brian.

There was nothing literal that stood between me and that word escaping my pursed lips, and yet there it sat in my throat, wanting to come out but unable to.

Full clarity on knowing that, in order for me to move forward and release this people pleasing trait, I had to just say that one word.

Paralyzed.

"But Brian doesn't like chicken?"

"Brian actually hates chicken?"

"I can tolerate having steak tonight but I really hate steak!"

"What if I say chicken and Brian is upset with me for picking chicken? What if I ruin his dinner because of this choice?"

"Why did he have to ask me this question? Why couldn't he just pick?"

Brian stood staring at me, trying to understand what was going on and completely unable to relate to me in that moment.

And so I took a deep breath and decided to jump over that wall. "Chicken," I whispered softly with head bowed and silent tears streaming down my cheeks which I didn't want him to see.

I felt like I was in physical pain and the discomfort was growing.

Absolute insanity, you might be thinking if you can't relate to this. But if you can, I suspect by now you are tallying the number of times you have stood before that wall, one hand placed firmly on it, knowing that you just needed to get to the other side with a few choice words.

Yet instead, you opted to step back and away, because the fear of the climb was overwhelming and it was simply easier to go along with what they said or wanted.

Do you have a wall of your own?

Is it large grey bricks that are one foot deep and that are covered with moss and moisture like mine?

Is it a wall that forms in your throat at the base of your neck where it traps the words that you actually want to say and locks them there?

Whatever your wall looks like, I can guarantee you I know how it feels as it suffocates you and builds up further people pleasing patterns because of its threat to harm you.

That day, standing there in the grocery store, was the first time I became fully aware of that wall, the one that I had erected through imaginary scenarios of "what ifs."

That was the day I took my first petrified leap over it.

Purposefully choosing to start small with something that was rather innocuous in order to prove to myself that I could do it.

What happened after blurting out that word "chicken" was rather life changing, to be honest. The realizations set in of just how often I found myself in that same scenario, witholding my most simplistic of choices based on unfounded fears and the need to please others.

The first jump was a challenge, but once I was on the other side, I realized that I now had positive proof: If I could do it once, I could do it again!

The journey continued, starting with the smaller decisions and choices, climbing to the deeper layer of situations that I held in.

Soon I realized that I had been making everything from dinner decisions to business decisions based on pleasing the other person involved.

There were times I stood on the inside of the wall and it grew to be closer to 40 feet tall. During those times, I can honestly admit that there were still situations I people pleased in.

Moments where I knew that I wanted to choose "X" but I chose "Y" instead. During the early days, I didn't feel ready for all the steps at once, but I did take note of them. Never allowing myself to make the same people pleasing decision twice.

Essentially, I got one free pass on a situation or experience, but after that, "no excuses" was the policy.

That 20 foot wall wasn't real.

It was the imaginary force keeping me from the life I wanted and had always envisioned, so I knew I had to become skilled at scaling it.

Now, five years later, that wall has long since been taken down completely.

On occasion, a pebble might get in my way that I have to kick out of my path, but that is essentially the degree of people pleaser left within me.

As you sit digesting this and applying to your own life in reflection, ask yourself how often you come up against that wall?

Once awareness has set in to that, remember that this is a journey and even the best rock climbers needed practice.

One doesn't start by scaling the heights of Mount Everest.

One starts by becoming practiced and efficient and scaling the smaller ones and learning along the way.

Pick a place to start today and commit to breaking the walls down that have formed around you over years.

Those walls lock you in, holding you back from your wants, dreams, desires, and goals.

It just takes that first leap... the other side is where living starts to happen.

** *Start Living Now* **

Pause for a moment and feel this chapter. Don't feel it for my journey but for yours and answer these questions.

~ Imagine your wall. Paint the picture in descriptive words. What does it look and feel like? The more descript you are the better able you will be to identify it when it is surrounding you.

~ When that wall is around you what do you feel physically in your body?

~ What situations in your life currently do you experience the presence of this wall?

~ Pick one situation and commit to leaping over the wall, start small and build proof that you can.

"Invisible Walls Built From Fear Are Only As Strong As Our Commitment To Maintain Them"

www.TheIconicMom.com

Go to The Iconic Mom and get access to more information, resources, tools and free downloads today.

Start Living The Way You Would Tell Your Kids To.

The Indifference Game

in-dif-fer-ence

noun

1) lack of interest, concern or sympathy
2) lack of concern, unconcern, disinterest, lack of interest, lack of enthusiasm, apathy, nonchalance, insouciance

What does it mean to be indifferent?

As per the definition above, it seems pretty straightforward, doesn't it?

As I prepared to write this chapter, I pulled up this definition so that I could shape my own thoughts on the matter based on the lessons that indifference and people pleasing played in my own life.

I did not intend to include the actual definition in the book but after reading it, laughing out loud, and chuckling at my own past disillusion, I knew it was essential.

Flash back to the top of this page and read it again.

I suspect if I were to take a random poll on the definition of the word "indifferent," a potential 10 out of 10 people would view it as an postion in life that is not serving.

Yet.

Several years ago I cloaked my world in indifference and stood by the notion with pride that it was something of value.

The chuckle came earlier when I realized that the one word I connected to value was "nonchalance" and, while I still view that as a serving quality, I have come to realize over the past few years just how much of a story this was to serve my people pleasing ways.

One of the greatest vices of a people pleaser is the absolute inability to make decisions easily and with little contemplation.

Flash back to the grocery story and the "chicken or steak?" dilemma of 2010. One would have thought that I was the President of the United States seated in the Situation Room trying to navigate whether or not to launch an attack on another country.

What do we do when we are faced with situations that unsettle us?

Our unconscious kicks in and provides us great coping strategies that may seemingly serve us in the moment but, down the road of life, end up coming back to bite us in the rear.

Unbeknownst to me until many years later, this is the exact road map that my unconscious chose to cope with these threatening decisions of life.

And so the "indifference game" began.

Rewind to the days of being a single mom. Life was all about finding balance between being the best mom I could, a entrepreneur, and somehow navigating the course of reconnecting with the "self" that I no longer knew from my past.

What little free time I was able to grab in those years became an essential part of my journey to today, and it was often spent with Jeremy.

Jeremy, whom I met just prior to my divorce when he was on bended knee greeting me.

Perhaps that sounds like quite the exaggerated display for a greeting but that described Jeremy well, abundant with love and gratitude that he and I shared space in this world.

Our first meeting came one afternoon when I waltzed into the resto-bar that he was managing to meet a few friends.

He swooned at our introduction, got on one knee and quipped that "a woman like you deserves a greeting as such."

A cheesy pick-up line would be the obvious de facto assumption of such a display, and yet the look in his big brown eyes as he gazed up from his spot on the ground spoke to me in a very different way.

I knew that this man in front of me would come to be one of my most trusted confidants, a person who I could lean on with my deepest of vulnerabilities. I knew he would change my life and forever be a part of my soul, no matter which way our ships steered us in.

Here I sit some seven years later from that first encounter and my heart still swells at the reality of how very true my instincts were about Jeremy.

I was as fragile as a woman could be when the universe brought him to me.

A wounded heart from a marriage that ended after years of angst and pain.

Moving forward in life with trepidation of trust and most certainly not prepared to let anyone in too close to my heart.

Protection was key. Back then I would argue it was essential, however much of a story that might be reflecting back.

The vow to myself I made shortly after my marriage ended and I met Jeremy was that I was never going to love again.

Of course that was a bullshit coping mechanism for an ego and heart that was bruised and in repair.

The vow was short-lived.

While my love for Jeremy isn't the "romantic" kind, it is that kind of soul love that overwhelms you in a beautiful way because you know that this person is a part of you.

The indifference game... he was the first to bring it to the surface and hold that ornate mirror up in front of me, causing a forced pause.

While you might have been thinking that I ran this chapter off track, the intention was purposeful. The relationship background is essential to demonstrate the bond and trust that resided between the two of us and how, while I was in the most delicate state of my life, he started to show me the potential of how this indifference game would be my fate.

A fate that I didn't truly want.

The Irish pub that we were in was loud, the music from the stage filling every space of its square footage.

We were in one of the two places that Jeremy and I could be found if we were out, in the middle of the dance floor totally in sync, dancing to whatever the current tune was booming out of the speakers.

While some of the details of the scene that followed are a little foggy some seven years later, the emotion of the moment hasn't escaped me.

A young woman walked by and gave me a compliment. The words she used are lost on me at this moment because I was in the middle of playing the indifference game shortly thereafter.

I politely accepted the compliment, but then she followed it up with a question that without a doubt was an opinion-based one.

Without hesitation, I shrugged my shoulders and coyly quipped, "It doesn't really matter to me; I am totally indifferent." With my nonchalant tone and cloak of taking life by the fly, I smiled.

The young woman persisted: "Are you really indifferent, or is that just what you keep telling yourself because you don't really have an opinion of your own."

The room closed around me, the music muffled, and I took on the poise of a cat rearing its back up in defense.

Jeremy witnessed all of this and, in his natural protective nature over me, put his hand on the small of my back to offer reassurance while he informed the young girl that she was "way off."

Later that night, which had turned to early morning, Jer and I had relocated our dancing feet to the patio and were comfortably nestled into our common conversational tones.

"You know she's right, don't you?"

Enter the background story of why trust with this man was so important.

I looked at him with what I am sure were puppy dog sad eyes, coupled with the likely want for him to simply cuddle me instead of sharing his thoughts.

The truth is cutting when you aren't prepared to hear it and, as this beautiful soul held up a mirror for me to glance into, I peeked just long enough to see the reflection but quickly averted my eyes because I wasn't yet ready to accept how the indifference game was simply another one of my traits of people pleasing.

Reaching for my hand to offer me a point of physical contact and safety, he started to speak in his ever stoic and intelligent grace that he possessed.

"Nonchalance or indifference is nothing more than a really pleasant way of masking the realities that lay beneath the surface, angel. You are so quick to ensure that everyone else is happy and you have lost so much of who you are in the last few years that you quite literally don't hold an opinion of your own.

"You mask it as a free-spirited nature, but this is going to come back to bite you in that perfect ass of yours.

"I love you darling, I always will; but I had to share this with you."

Who would have guessed that, years after that summer night, I would reflect upon that conversation with great clarity and realize just how right he was?

Piece by piece over the years that followed, I found myself in countless scenarios where I was playing the MVP on "team indifference."

Decisions of great magnitude, opinions of intense emotion, and daily musings that I left unattended to by my own considerations.

Indifference saved me from the potential pain that my people pleaser perceived would come if I made a decision or levied and opinion that was not of preferential choice.

Indifference allowed me to veil the coping strategy in what I perceived at the time as a characteristic of a free spirit.

It wasn't until some years later in my own journey of becoming aware of my people pleasing ways that I came to understand that this was merely another layer of this persona that I had adopted over the course of my life span.

Call it what you want.

A nonchalant attitude.

An indifference choice.

A 'laissez-faire" approach to life.

Distill it down to one single question:

Have you adopted this as a scarcity or abundance philosophy?

Confusion reigned on that one for me for what felt like decades. The mask was on so firmly that my unconscious had convinced me this story was real.

Peeling it back took practice and abandoning the indifference game required a lot of internal work.

However, when the floodgates opened on this one, it was a tidal wave of reality that swept across my life and started to wash out all the remnants of the team that I had erected around me.

The shrug of my shoulders, the cute little smile I formed with my mouth, and the words "I don't really care" no longer were a quotidian habit.

By now I suspect you have unearthed the parts of your life that you play this game in and have started to become aware of the truth that it is really a losing battle you are playing.

The change is a simple one to start evoking immediately.

Next time those shoulders are seeking their habitual path to your ears in a perfected shrug or your lips are rotely about to form in order to say "I don't care," simply stop.

Stop and ask yourself one truly valuable question that will change your world:

"What do I really want?"

** Start Living Now **

Pause for a moment and feel this chapter. Don't feel it for my journey but for yours and answer these questions.

~ Take the time to sit and really think about this. Consider all the people you interact with daily. Do you play the indifference game? And if so with who?

~ Next time you catch yourself in the game ask yourself silently, "What do I really want?"

"Indifference In Scarcity Will Leave You Without Abundance Of Self"

www.TheIconicMom.com

Go to The Iconic Mom and get access to more information, resources, tools and free downloads today.

Start Living The Way You Would Tell Your Kids To.

CARRIE CAMPBELL

The Perpetual Circle of People Pleasing

Think about your car.

You slide in behind the wheel, buckle your seat belt, and start the engine.

Your foot reaches for the gas pedal to begin moving you forward on your journey.

If you were to depress the pedal right to the ground, what would happen?

The car would buck forward in a fury and abrasively shake you.

A car doesn't get from 0 to 100 km an hour in the blink of an eye.

It is a process of gradual increases and strength of the engine working in harmony with all the other parts to get us to where we are headed.

People pleasing, I have come to learn, is not dissimilar.

It isn't a 0 to 100 km process that happens in the blink of an eye. It is process of gradual increase until we reach the destination.

Like all journeys, when we reach a destination, at some point we turn around and come back or go another way.

Visualize this as a people pleaser, a slow and steady climb that climaxes at a point and then starts all over again.

I call it the "circle of people pleasing" and it is one that I was trapped in on repeat for years, uncertain of how to get out of.

I found myself in the 150 km zone too many times and then watched as the journey would commence shortly thereafter, starting at 0 and rapidly reaching the danger zone.

The danger zone of maximal speeds or, in this case, maximal emotion is often what people see as the true cause for concern. However, as I drove down this road of awareness, it came quickly to light that in fact that danger zone wasn't the problem at all.

It was the collision that happened after meandering over the yellow line too many times.

The fatal moment that you wished you had been more cautious in preventing rather than having to clean up once implosion occurred.

With the common sense knowledge that, if a car doesn't go from 0 to 150, neither do I, I set out to uncover how to recognize the patterns that got me into the 'danger zone.'

Perhaps the best place to start here would be by offering you a deeper understanding of this tumultuous state that I speak of, which, for the longest time, I blamed as the precipitating issue.

Feelings, thoughts, behaviors, and physical symptoms manifested during these torrid cycles, and yet it was a challenge to try to isolate any of them down to precisely that.

The experiences in the "danger zone" were intense and tornado-like, but once the calm after the storm would settle in, I committed myself to become aware.

The feelings of guilt that took hold were the equivalent of the mattress layers in the classic fairytale "The Princess and The Pea."

Stacked one on top of the other, the layers of guilt would lead to deep shame and embarrassment that I had even escalated to the crash in the first place.

It was a nightmarish bed to have made for myself and many times I wished I could run from it, but as the age-old saying goes, "If you make your bed you must lie in it."

The emotion, of course, was derived from the thoughts that played in my head like a young child who was in the perpetual state of "why?" Over and over again, my mind would tell me the things I needed to hear least.

"Why did you do this again? You are such an idiot!"

"You don't deserve to have anyone's compassion when you act this way!"

"He is going to leave you if you don't stop this!"

They would circle over and over, nagging me, driving me deeper into the emotional state of paralysis, only adding more mattresses to my bed.

Of course, what happens when you combine feelings and thoughts? You end up with behaviors that manifest by the boatloads and physical symptoms in your body that threaten to render you ill.

Tears would run a never-ending stream starting at my eyelids and pooling in the crooks of my clavicles.

My breath would shorten and my chest constrict against the unnatural state of emotion that was ongoing in the moment.

Like a small wet dog standing in the rain outside a store waiting for his owner, I would tremble, the inside-out kind of tremble.

Isolation is what I sought, so I would remove myself from the immediate surroundings of all those who loved me (after all, I didn't deserve them anyway).

However, isolation was far too suffocating to tolerate for any length of time, so I would ping-pong back and forth, trying to seek comfort from people who, no matter what they did, couldn't match the intoxicating overdose of emotion that was consuming me.

Apologies by the masses went out like the updates on my Instagram account.

Outreaches of love to show people I still cared were a desperate plea for me to rid the guilt that was choking me out.

"Want me to give you a foot rub tonight?"

"Can I pick you up anything if I go out that you might need?"

It was what you would call the "head-on collision" of a lifetime that shuts down highways for hours.

The pile up that you have to clean up.

But.

I got tired of cleaning it up and knew that it was in my hands to remedy.

I have told this story hundreds of times to my mindset coaching clients all over the world and not once have I ever found someone who to some degree can't relate.

Perhaps the extreme emotion and the thoughts manifest differently for you.

Perhaps you slam doors and break things and withdraw instead of cry.

I will hedge my bets, however risky it might be, that you can relate to this 150 km hour zone.

Either in your current life or in your past, you have known a moment like this.

Hard to ignore those moments of intensity that shake your being for days. Looking back, it is rather obvious to state that this wasn't the starting point, this was the climax of a series of trigger points along the way.

How did I unravel the circle that was so destructive to my life?

This is the question you are likely asking right now.

The answer is quite simple in philosophy but takes practice in the practical form.

I accepted that the only person who could create change to this was me.

I became aware of the little nuances of each stage on the path to the collision.

I took accountability for my actions and thus was able to create change.

I began to adapt my world and my actions to line up with what I wanted, not the disastrous patterns that I had created.

Over the next chapter, I will introduce you to each stage of my own personal people pleasing cycle.

Know this: we are all different and our patterns are not necessarily aligned. These were mine, so take from them and uncover yours as they are your one and only path to freedom.

Your starting point is simply the point of highest impact; start by becoming aware at that point today.

Don't look to get to the core of the onion before peeling off all the layers.

Get behind the wheel, start the engine and make this drive one that doesn't land you in the ditch.

** Start Living Now **

Start becoming aware of your IMPACT point in order to create change. Think about the most recent situation where you were in the 150 km an hour zone and answer these questions:

~ What were you feeling emotionally?

~ What were you physically experiencing?

~ What were you thinking?

~ What were your behaviors?

Become aware of these in order to recognize early warning signs. When you experience these moments remind yourself that this state of being does not serve you.

"If You Never Go Within You

Will Always go Without"

~ Brian Grasso

www.TheIconicMom.com

Go to The Iconic Mom and get access to more information, resources, tools and free downloads today.

The Characters of People Pleasing

Let me introduce you to Patty, Rhonda, Valerie, Debbie, and Gene.

These lovely ladies used to be my arch-nemeses until I realized that they would teach me more about myself than I ever knew possible.

All these ladies played a part in the circle of my people pleasing ways. They played off of one another and at times would gang up to make my life more difficult than I felt was reasonable.

Perhaps an introduction to their full names will help you understand the intricacy of how they all, for some time, owned my life.

Patty the People Pleaser.

Rhonda the Resentful.

Valerie the Victim.

Debbie the Defender.

Gene the Guilty.

For the longest time I walked around with the belief that I was all these things. That my personality was laden with these negative feelings, thoughts, and behaviors.

Then one day I realized I was not any of these things things. I had merely adopted all these characters into my world as what I refer to as the "fallout effect" of being a people pleaser.

As I peeled back the layers from the destructive state of guilt that I described to you in the previous chapter, I started to uncover the trigger effect of all of these so-called characters. Each and every one of them spurring the next one on.

It was obvious that Gene the Guilty was the most intense and therefore the most apparent and easiest to pick up on, but once I had accepted that there was no way this could be the o km/hour zone, I heightened my awareness, braced myself and walked "eyes wide open" into my own unconscious.

I loathed Gene the Guilty at first. Everything about her made me angry. The way that she would lash out at her loved ones, cry for hours upon hours, leaving my face puffy and swollen for days, and the feelings that she used to perpetuate in me following an implosion.

Then one day, in a quiet moment of reflection gazing out my bedroom window, I came to the decision, however doubtful I might have been, that as much as this wasn't me, I needed to take ownership and accountability.

Giving her a name, Gene, allowed me to disconnect from her being a part of my own character and released me from the shackles of her grip. The anger faded and the fight turned into more of a flow.

I embraced what she could teach me, if I only listened to her warning signs.

Listen I did and, when I paused the rampant emotion long enough to do that, the thread on the spool started to unravel, forging the path to freedom that I uncovered.

There I was perched at my stand up desk, clicking away on my keyboard with fury. I kept asking myself while shaking my head, "What just happened?"

Only a few short minutes ago I had been lost in the romance of my life, working beside my now husband and loving our co-created world.

How did the day turn on a dime and land into a place where tears were threatening to fall and my insides were trembling with anxiety, frustration and confusion.

I stood silently, trying to find clarity in the midst of the chaos of my emotions. My ego wanted to blame Brian, I was well aware of that, but my heart knew that wasn't accurate.

And so there I stood, contemplating and silent when the moment of clarity happened.

Picture that thread that is hanging on the edge of a shirt. It has been teasing your for days, begging for you to pull it and then when you do it simply starts to unravel with ease. An ease that is almost annoying because it is out of your control, it seems. At any point in time you can cut it off with a pair of scissors, but you are too inquisitive to not just keep gently tugging.

That is what happened to me that day when the circle of my people pleasing unravelled right before my eyes and the confusion gave way to clarity.

Within minutes, the road that I had travelled down so many times was so perfectly laid out right in front of me.

I had spent years in disdain of Gene the Guilty, but she wasn't the culprit that started the party of negativity. No, she was merely the innocent bystander in the corner waiting to get pulled into the crowd.

Patty, she was the one that started it all. Patty the People Pleaser and her pleasing, docile ways that were cloaked with the air of doing good and meaning well, she was the firestarter.

Then the rest of the negative party would follow, with Rhonda the Resentful coming up next to bat, followed by Valerie the Victim, Debbie the Defender, and the one who got the short end of the "blame" stick, Gene the Guilty.

What was it that day?

What catalyzed this pattern of disruption?

The answer is the most innocuous action one could possibly imagine.

As you read this next part, try to imagine your own life and the number of times you have found yourself in similar pattern.

The moment that brought me all this clarity started when Brian interrupted me to ask me a question.

We had both had our heads down working on something we were in the middle of creating. In true form to Brian's mind, he had an idea and wanted my input, so he interrupted me to ask me.

In true form to myself, I stopped everything that I was doing without pause for consideration and answered his question, thinking nothing of it.

Patty the People Pleaser was running that show. With complete disregard for what I might have been doing in the moment, she simply dropped it to give everything to the person who was in front of her.

The thing you have to understand about Patty is that she is the complete opposite of Gene. Calm and not loud. Gentle and not angry. Accommodating in love (or so I thought) and not vengeful. Her physical self doesn't react negatively and her thoughts don't even pause for a moment to consider.

You can see easily how this quiet lamb of a character could so easily monopolize a world.

It wasn't until about 30 minutes later that the effects of Patty made their appearance.

I needed something from Brian and without forethought interrupted him to ask.

Short and curt (or so my mind interpreted in the moment), he replied, "Not right now, I don't have time. Try not to interrupt me when I am working!"

My thoughts in that moment: "What the fuck?"

Resentful Rhonda was definitely a thinker. Her thoughts would rapid fire with almost a venom-like quality, giving way to emotions of frustration, anger, and disappointment. Her thoughts and emotions would spiral her into a place where her body felt like an electric charge was racing through it and her face would flush.

"Sure, it was fine when he interrupted me half an hour ago?"

'Does he not realize that he just did the same thing to me?"

"Why can't he extend the same thing back to me that I offered him?"

Rhonda would take hold of the energy in the room and in seconds it would become palpable to both of us.

Her huffy behavior and demeanour attracted Brian's attention immediately, begging the question from him, "What is wrong?"

Of course, Patty the People Pleaser was still present so the possibility of actually expressing what was going on in my head was an impossibility. Quipping a non-emotional "Nothing" had become my skill, which is exactly what I did that day before we both returned to our work.

Of course, at any point in time along the way, had I known all this, I could have interrupted the pattern of triggers which, after this day, I managed to do effectively.

However, this day was one of learning, and the process unfolded.

Putting my head back down, resentment dissipated some and Valerie took over. The closest comparison I could draw to Valerie the Victim would be that of Eeyore from the classic Winnie the Pooh children's books.

My shoulders would slump forward, face bleeding a frown that couldn't be lifted if someone did so with plastic surgery, and I simply sat and wallowed.

"How can he not see what just happened?"

The "woe is me" pity party took over and I sat mulling through my work, letting out purposeful sighs every few minutes in order to hopefully catch his attention and he would therefore ask me if there was something wrong.

I didn't realize any of that in the moment, clearly, because if I had, the situation wouldn't have continued down the path it was on.

Have you caught the irony yet that just a few minutes prior to Valerie taking over, Brian did ask me what was wrong?

My opportunity to express at any moment was there, but Resentful Rhonda was too feisty to want to share; she preferred the pissy state of being.

Minutes ticked by in this slow state of Eeyore-like behavior and, with each passing of 60 seconds on the clock, Victimized Valerie grew increasingly sourpussed in the face, sighing louder and willing him to look up.

When he didn't, the word, "Ummm..." followed by nothing escaped my lips as if controlled by a poltergeist.

Looking up, Brian asked, "What's up?"

As I type this out, what I see now as a ridiculous dance of my own ego roles, I laugh at the absolute circus that must have gone on in the kitchen that day.

"Oh no nothing, never mind."

"Okay." he said.

Valerie sunk deeper into my soul.

"Well maybe if you have a few seconds we can talk."

"Sure thing. What's up?" His nonchalant tone only aggravated me more and I teetered on the edge of eruption.

Then true to form, in an explosion of nonsensical verbal diarrhea, I started telling him everything that he did wrong. Like vomit spewing out of a child sick with a stomach virus, I threw up all over our day.

With a deer-in-headlights look about him, Brian paused long enough to let me calm down (or so he thought) before saying, "That is NOT what happened."

He pointed out all of the actualities, and Debbie the Defender came in, guns blazing, to counter each and every one.

Point, counterpoint.

That is what happened in an exhausting dance marathon that had lost its merit long ago.

Then without fail, when the circle of people pleasing was near complete, Gene the Guilty made her way into the kitchen.

Sobbing tears of apologies for messing up the day.

Claiming hormonal surges, bad sleep, and a headache as today's source problem.

Begging for forgiveness like a child who just got caught in a lie.

I crumbled.

I relented.

I didn't know why, however, because inside me at that point, that day in the kitchen, I was still sure I was right.

Yet as I stood there in silence at my computer screen when the thread started to pull I came to realize it was all me.

The entire exchange was rooted in my actions and patterns and it all started with people pleasing.

Clarity came in like a gust of wind on a winter's day, offering the same chill of realization that I was getting slapped into wakefulness.

I didn't want to stop what I was doing to answer Brian's question.

That is it!

That is the moment that catalyzed it all.

Unable to express, "Sorry honey, can you wait a minute."

Seven words that could change the course of events that unfolded that day.

Instead I did what every people pleaser does.

I tabled my own needs and wants to tend to those of the people around me and, without knowing, I unconsciously built the expectation that he should and would do the same.

That somehow he would see my grand gesture of being there for him as something that required a reciprocal action.

When, a few minutes later my unconscious expectation was not met, the circle began with Rhonda the Resentful leading the charge.

WOW!

That was all I could summon as I sat back in my chair and chuckled at my own circus that had just played out all its acts within a 30-minute window.

Awareness kept flooding in and I realized just how many times this particular scene played out and how much resentment I had been holding onto, not realizing that the change was in my hands the entire time.

On that particular day, the circle stopped. It has never reached the guilt phase again because I became a master at catching and adapting to all the levels of acceleration along the way.

However, I want to point out how the circle would complete itself in the past.

As a people pleaser, guilt is, I suspect, the monster that perpetuates the circle.

Once guilt sets in, the immediate action is to start pleasing again in order to make amends and thus it starts all over.

The scene that played out that day was tornado-like quick, but other times it would be days or months that it would carry on, moving through the stages.

I do not believe that your circle is the same as mine, but I do know that there is a circle for everyone who is a people pleaser.

This one day.

This one moment.

Changed my life forever as I started to understand the process that unfolded and rendered me right back to where I began.

As you read this, I suspect you saw traces of yourself or someone you know. Draw awareness to the circle because the only way to break a circle is to interrupt it along the way.

*** Start Living Now ***

In order to move out of the impact zone you have to become aware of your circle of reaction. Where does it start and stop? How is it triggered? This is a mindful task and involves self-awareness and reflection. For the purpose of the journey start here:

~ Identify the top 3 most intense, frequent or debilitating roles that exist in your circle of reaction.

~ Give them each a name and list their characteristics.

~ Become aware of when these characters are the ones in control of your actions.

"Your Ego Can Teach You Much About Yourself If You Learn To Listen Instead Of React"

www.TheIconicMom.com

Go to The Iconic Mom and get access to more information, resources, tools and free downloads today.

Start Living The Way You Would Tell Your Kids To...

CARRIE CAMPBELL

The Childhood People Pleaser

In full disclosure, I don't think it is ever serving to ask ourselves, "Why we are the way we are?"

For a period of time I was quite certain I was a people pleaser because of my past abusive relationships as an adult. I soon realized, however, that people pleasing has been laced into my being for much longer.

Able to track it all the way back to my childhood, I have to be honest that I am not quite sure I can recall a time that this trait was not a part of me.

Why it was a trait didn't matter and I will explain that fully later on in this book, but the fact that it was affecting my life for as long as I could remember was definitely an eye-opening experience.

As a child I could recall being the one in the house who was always trying to make peace with any sort of conflict that arose.

The middle man (child) between my parents on the very odd occasion that they fought. Willing them with my quiet prayers at night for them to stop and make up would be followed the next day by accommodating behaviors, trying to bridge the distance between them.

The rock for my mother who suffered from years of Agoraphobia and would lean on me for support at the tender age of 13. My soul is one that heals, this I know, but I realized looking back that I would drop everything to be what she needed.

The examples are many and the spaces of time between them vary.

As I was reflecting on all this in preparation for sharing my stories with you, helping you forge a new day for yourself, one story stood out above all of them.

Partially because, even now as a grown woman, this particular experience can be brought to mind and conjure the exact emotion I felt that day.

Mostly, however, because I realize that this is the type of scenario that could have led to a different path for me and I was somewhat shocked to realize that this moment that was etched into my sexuality for years was a product of me people pleasing.

At the age of 8 I was not much unlike who I am now as a 37-year-old woman.

A Tinkerbell of a girl who floated more than walked. Who woke up smiling and went to bed singing. A girl who had very little concern for anything other than what she was going to do to her Barbie's hair that day.

A free spirit in the grandest definition of one who simply loved wholly and with all of herself.

So it was painful. Dreadfully painful for me as I lay in bed one night with the knot of disgust in my belly, the feelings of shame coursing through me, and repulsed by something that I didn't quite understand.

The air was hot and humid that day, as it often was in the middle of July. I bubbled with excitement when my mom gave me permission to spend the day at my friend's house.

I grabbed my bathing suit, jumped on my bike, and headed over to her house.

We spent the day in the usual pattern at her house. Swimming, laughing, eating, and playing.

The simplicity of children and the joy of a hazy summer day.

So why was I lying in bed hours later that night feeling an internal pain I hadn't experienced before?

The answer, I know now, is because people pleasing was at play and, like many times over the course of the next years of my life, it dictated my action and decisions.

"Can we play a new game?" she asked.

We were in her bedroom and I can recall that it was dark because the drapes were drawn and the door was closed.

Her mom had stepped out to the store so we were alone in her large home.

"Sure, what game?" I quipped, always eager to try new things.

"It's a game you can't tell anyone about. A secret game. It will be our game only. Do you trust me?"

My ability to read people and situations energetically was finely tuned even at that age and the hairs on my back immediately raised, while shadows of doubt and worry crept in.

I felt trapped for some reason. Her mom wasn't home, the door was closed and the room felt small all of a sudden.

The clandestine tone of her voice and the secrecy of the game left me in a lurch of the unknown.

My immediate thought was echoed in my mom's voice reminding me "We don't keep secrets in this house." Already cause for alarm.

"Um, okay but how do we play it?" With a shaky voice I asked and, even as the words poured out, I didn't know why I was saying them when I wanted to really run and say "no thanks."

"I can't tell you, it is easier to show you."

"Ummmm, okay....." again I said. Why was I doing that?

As I type this, goosebumps appear on my own arms. Not because this memory is one that still holds any degree of pain for me but because it is so vivid, so real that I can feel the pull of being trapped there that day.

Watching as I agreed to things that I didn't want to do.

She told me to lie on the bed on my back and close my eyes.

I complied.

She told me to keep my eyes closed as she got ready.

I complied, but not without my belly doing a somersault and threatening to turn over.

I heard her dresser drawer close and the rustling of clothing.

I knew in that moment this was sexual.

I didn't know much about sex at that age, but innately I knew that this is not what I should be feeling.

After all, my parents had had the "my body is nobody's body but mine" talk with me a million times.

My heart raced as she walked closer to me and told me we had to be quiet in case her mom came home.

I swallowed the bile in my throat, quietly wished my mommy was there, and squeezed my lids tighter.

The bed depressed at the foot and I knew she was getting closer to me.

Time stopped and then came back in a flash when I realized that she had spread my legs and, still in my bathing suit, I could feel her lie on top of me.

There was something in her own bathing suit at the point where her own legs met. A round hard object that I came to learn was a bunch of balled-up socks.

She started to move against me with what I now know was sensual movement beyond her years.

With each undulating move of her 8-year-old hips, I was begging for someone to come save me from this experience that my mom had taught me about.

"My body's nobodys.... body but mine....."
The words trailed off.

I finally got the gall to say, "I don't think I really like this game."

Up until that moment, I attributed it to childhood innocence and play of curiosity

"I have to practice this game," she said. "My Daddy told me if I don't practice it I will get in trouble."

Right there: "I will get in trouble."

I remember my thoughts exactly like I'm reciting the alphabet. "Well I don't want her to get in trouble," echoed in my head.

I shrugged my shoulders, swallowed again, and said "okay."

The details from this point forward are not needed as the graphics of the experience are not the point of this story.

My first sexual experience was one that left scars for some time on me.

Feelings of violation and disgust.

Perceptions of weakness that I allowed this to happen.

Years later in my twenties, I still was unable to watch movies where sexual scenes were violent or involuntary without feeling nausea swarm into my belly.

Yes, I was a child and I was an innocent victim of the situation. I still wonder to this day if her father was the root of this game or if that was a strategy to get me to embark on the game train.

I don't blame her. I don't hold anger over her. That would leave me a victim of my circumstances.

Of course I didn't realize it that night as I walked down the hallway to where my mom was sitting watching TV with tears streaming down my face, but as I started on my own journey of people pleasing awareness I realize that even this was a moment of that mask.

"I don't want her to get into trouble."

Taking responsibility for someone else.

Not able to say no.

Fear of what would happen to her if I did, not to myself.

A complete disregard for my own wants.

Classic people pleasing behavior written all over that.

As you read these words, if you find yourself gravitating towards thoughts that perhaps are categorizing this as an over-exaggeration of the moment, I will ask you this.

If you have a child, think about him or her. If you don't, think about a child you know.

As much as I wanted to look back upon this moment and deflect the reality of what it was, I couldn't because of my own daughter.

A spitting image of her mother in heart and soul.

Eager to please everyone and make sure that everyone's heart is happy, even at the cost of her own.

I think about her because, from the early days of her life, I was able to pick up on her own apparently natural tendencies to people please and realize that, if my situation had happened to her, I would want to do everything to retrace the steps and change it.

The words people pleasing are familiar to her now and she knows that taking care of herself has to always come first.

Intent on ingraining in her the life lessons I learned much later than I wish I had, I make sure to live my life "eyes wide open."

I don't profess to think it is imperative to go back to your childhood to trace the roots of your own people pleasing tendencies.

As a matter of fact, I don't think it is necessary at all. I didn't go looking for this moment of clarity; it found me when I opened my mind to taking accountability and accepting that much of the road that was laid in front of me was at my own hand and had been for a very long time.

Let this chapter speak to you in whatever way you choose.

Perhaps a reflection of how you are parenting if you have kids.

A consideration of how long people pleasing behaviors have been impacting your life.

Or.

The reality that these behaviors can affect both the big and small things in life.

Never underestimate the power of awareness. The wider we open our eyes the more we see and the greater change we can create.

** *Start Living Now* **

Emotionally this was the most challenging chapter to write. Not because of it taking me back in time but because of the reminder of how many situations over my life I have found myself in where people pleasing dictated. I don't mean "chicken or steak" type situations.

I allowed myself to feel this chapter more deeply in order to instill in you how profound an effect people pleasing can have on your life. Feel now as you move through these reflections.

~ Spend 15 minutes sitting and feeling this chapter and my story, allow your thoughts to go to your own life. Can you think of a time or a situation that carries a similar emotional weight?

~ Allow yourself to let this awareness in, feel it, in order to accept that you can and must create change for yourself.

"Your Problem Isn't Your Past,
It Is That You're Allowing Your
Past To Become Your Future"

www.TheIconicMom.com

Go to The Iconic Mom and get access to more information, resources, tools and free downloads today.

The Mother Teresa Syndrome, Superwoman Cape, and Other Masks of a People Pleaser

The masks we wear are the truth we know.

Our world becomes what we believe and the stories that we tell ourselves.

Over the years, I have worn many masks as a people pleaser and veiled myself with many capes and cloaks to help support the story that I was not creating a deficit in my life.

The masks and the capes rotated in a given year, moment, or experience, depending on which one was the best supporting role for me.

None of this was conscious, none of this was a choice of known action in the moment.

Our unconscious drives all our habits and actions of daily life, sometimes knowing up to six seconds before our conscious mind knows exactly what is going to be said or done.

99

Stop and think about the power of that statement.

Before you do what you do or say what you say, your unconscious has already made up its mind for you.

This is the exact reason that, as a Mindset Coach, the foundation I am always building with clients is unconscious awareness.

My conscious mind wasn't actively deciding to create a story that supported my inability to say no or to take care of myself first. It wasn't some master plan that I plotted out.

It was driven unknowingly from my unconscious, which was crafting it for me.

However, once I found awareness to it all, at that point the pen was in my hand to start drafting a new story.

Like many other tales of awareness you have read throughout these pages, I was rather blindsided when I came to full acceptance that these masks were nothing but a layer of protection.

Superwoman cape.

Supermom glory.

Mother Teresa syndrome.

Powerful words and names that brought to mind the immediate image of feminine strength of body and mind, not to mention a heart of gold.

Words that had been tied to me for years, since I was a child, and had developed into my self-fulfilling prophecy.

Here is the thing: I still would define myself by those adjectives above. The difference is that they drive inward first before being propelled outward.

Let me help you look in the mirror and uncover the masks that you don to protect yourself from the truth.

The masks that, while pretty and elaborate, are only supporting a story that truly doesn't serve your greater vision for the life you know you want.

The Mother Teresa syndrome was my crutch and my favorite mask of all time to hide behind.

A woman who lived a life of service to others and died with a legacy that perhaps will never be matched in comparison.

A woman who gave freely of herself and without greed.

A woman who in my eyes, as a child growing up, was "healing the world."

The parallels were easy for my subconscious to draw in the intricately carved story of my people pleasing support system.

Since the tender age of three, all I ever wanted to do was help people.

Heal sadness and sorrow. Release people from pain and suffering.

All while leading a life free of greed and in love for others.

Beautiful, isn't it?

Again, the truth is that I still live in the service of others.

My heart is still set to the default of wanting to deliver the world from pain and sadness. Ridding the world of grief and torment and creating a better place for my children, your children, our children.

The difference now, however, is that I have removed the shroud of bullshit that I veiled myself in, convincing me that I was selfish if I put myself first.

I gave all of myself with nothing left for me in the past.

I walked around with the mindset that I could fix everyone and that it was also my responsibility to.

Sleepless nights were on the rise ten years ago, as was my anxiety level when people needed me.

As a counsellor for children with special needs and teenagers suffering from severe psychosocial issues, not only did I make them my priority but I took on every ounce of their pain.

Into my heart and my body.

I cried tears of sadness on a weekly basis for their pains.

I slept few hours as I crafted ways to service them better.

I dropped everything when a parent called needing to talk to me in a panic, regardless of the time.

I missed family events to respond to last minute emergencies.

I gave all of myself but, in doing so, I lost myself.

Fatigued, stressed, looking ten years older than I was and with no time for myself.

But... I was Mother Teresa in the making, so this was an essential part of the process, so I told myself.

In conversation with people, I would act as though I had no choice and quip with laugher as I spouted, "It's Mother Teresa syndrome, I can't help it."

I would receive heartfelt praise and blessings from all that would listen.

"You are so patient, I could never do what you do!"

"You have the heart of gold... the world needs more like you."

I won't belabor the truth, it felt good.

My praises were being sung, my mask was being recognized as valiant, and thus I was sitting in reward of my offerings.

Every people pleaser sits somewhere in the delusion that they don't care about this praise and generosity of compliments, but it only serves to feed the beast that is masked in kindness.

Offering a momentary sentiment that carries the gestures of giving completely of oneself, moving forward to an acceptable state of being.

Like every Band-Aid, however, no matter how firmly affixed to the skin it is, eventually the sentiment falls flat and, just like the Band-Aid losing its adherence, you are left with two options: reapply a new bandage or leave the wound open to heal.

The temporary boost that my ego received in hearing the words shared in reverence would always fade away, leaving me feeling resentful that my dedication was somewhat unappreciated.

During these moments is when the mask would come out in full force, covering the anxiety, frustration, fatigue, and resentment and trumpeting all the good that I was doing in the world in order to receive yet another hit of the drug of compliment cocktails which my ego was used to.

To serve authentically is beautiful.

To love wholly and freely is sublime.

To give without expectation of return is rewarding.

People pleasers veil themselves in the lies that this is who they are and that the reason they do what they do is to give of themselves.

Until the bandage falls off, the self-acceptance falters, and the seeking of validation ensues.

There is a balance to be found where you can love others, give to others, share with others, and serve others without having to cloak yourself in a shroud of fallacies.

How?

Is the likely question you are asking right now.

How do you free yourself of these shackles that you have locked on yourself, that put you in a place where you feel choice is no longer yours?

How do you prioritize yourself when the guilt and the shame consume every ounce of you?

The first part of this has already happened without you realizing it, as you have quietly flipped the pages of this book.

Seeking awareness and acceptance that this is you.

Finding comfort in knowing this was me in the past and that I am going to share with you further pieces of my own journey that helped me move from pleasing others to prioritizing me.

The Four Pillars of Change

As a Mindset Master Coach and Mom Mentor, my forever place to start any journey lies in the foundation of best mindset practices.

Coaching women and moms worldwide, you can likely imagine that the span of life circumstance that I am navigating changes with each individual.

However, no matter the desired outcome and without question applicable to that of a people pleaser craving release from one's own self-created prison, the starting point is mindset.

It is the foundation from which all things will grow. It is the seed planted in the soil that will lead to the birth of a beautiful blossom.

Why are you a people pleaser?

The answer is, "I don't really care!"

What I care about is that people pleasing is holding you back, and uncovering how that happens and how it affects your life is where I really want to stay.

I have had countless clients over my nearly 20 years in the coaching industry express to me their fatigue and impatience with spending yet another visit to their therapist where they sit and trace back the steps of their life to find out "why?"

The frustration in these clients is palpable, the annoyance growing with each cheque that they write, each 60-minute session that ticks by, and each year of their life that they are not moving forward.

We can't go back and change the past.

It is done.

We can't go back and really understand why something happened.

We only have our perspective, and that is likely skewed by interpretations and memory failures.

All that I have or you have or she has is today and the promise or hope of a better tomorrow.

As you nod your head reading this and perhaps even offer a fist pump to the ceiling, your emotions are about to fall flat.

Why?

Likely because all you know is to ask "why?" And if you don't ask why, how can you possibly move forward?

The answer is simple, the execution easy, if a choice is made.

The four pillars of mindset that I teach to all the women who I am blessed to walk with in life as well as the four pillars that started to release me from my own people pleasing ways are about to be yours.

Acceptance.

Awareness.

Accountability.

Adaptation.

Four words.

Four actionable points.

A life of change.

** *Start Living Now* **

Over the remainder of this book, condensed into four chapters I am giving you the starting line you need to begin running the journey.

In this page of reflection I ask you not to complete a task but to open you mind to what you are about to read.

To recognize that these very pages are the foundation I use to change lives every day as a Mindset Master Coach.

While I have offered you all that I can in these pages I want to give you more. Are you ready for change? Are you ready to create a world free of chains?

Go to www.TheIconicMom.com and click on the button for a free Soul Call. It's not enough for me to offer you this and to not connect in the real world.

Click on the link, fill in the form and then I personally will connect with you to schedule a free 10 minute Soul Call with me.

Two minutes now that will offer you ten minutes that can change your life.

The Worth of Acceptance

Acceptance is the first cog in the wheel of four pillars and it is a critical one that, if we choose to avoid it, will come back to bite us in the end.

As you have read through the pages of this book, you have walked through the intimate journeys of my own life with me.

Perhaps you have shed tears of empathy or pain of your own, found moments of clarity, or experienced an elusive "a-ha" moment.

You have laughed with me, cried with me, walked with me, and related with me, and now here you are at the fork in the road and the spotlight is about to be turned on to your life.

Idling at the intersection, you toggle between the indicator on the right and the one on the left.

The indicator that sits next to the driver's side door on the left is your escape route, the easy way out (for now), and the path that you have traveled until now.

If you are thinking about going that way, it might be because anxiety is building in your chest and you are fearing the reality that now is "go time" and you have to change.

This might be the part of this book where you start to claim you lose interest and find yourself wanting to put it down.

That is the left hand turn that, no matter how you slice it, is yours to take if you so choose.

But the indicator on the right: that is a whole different story.

If you choose to go right, your only escape route from the car would be to climb over the passenger seat, which might be cumbersome and annoying but rewarding when you find freedom.

The path on the right is the new path. The one that you can start charting today and will lead you to the freedom you crave, the happiness you desire, and finally shedding the role of the people pleaser who is pretending you have it all.

This is where acceptance starts to settle in.

Truly accepting means that you recognize authentically that this path you have walked for the duration of your life can be undone.

That the likelihood of it actually being a permanent fixed state is not anything more permanent than a marker before it is doused in nail polish remover to rid the lines.

Acceptance means you realize that, while you have been walking as a people pleaser your entire life, perhaps it does not have to remain your future, that you have choice.

Your behaviors are nothing more than a result of the subconscious drivers that are enacting them.

Recall the statistic that blew your mind: your subconscious mind knows up to 6 seconds before your conscious mind knows exactly what it is going to do or say.

Learn to change your subconscious, and learn to stop people pleasing.

Yes, it really is as simple as that.

I am not saying that you won't have to crawl over the stick shift, the center console, and the passenger seat to get there, but you will get there.

Before your thoughts turn to supporting evidence as to why you can't change this, because it is you and always has been you, yes I am that good that I can read you mind through a book.

I would like to offer you positive proof as to why it is possible.

Remember me?

That woman who sat in the corner of a kitchen clawing at her arms in anger and fury because people pleasing caused her to keep everything in.

The woman who stood like a child staring up at her husband in a grocery store, near panic attack because she couldn't decide what she wanted for dinner.

The woman who engaged in sexual games that left her feeling shamed for years because she didn't want her friend to get in trouble.

Remember me?

The people pleaser who almost lost her life to the sadness that engulfed her because of this "role" I played.

That was me.

And quite simply put, if I can do it, so can you.

All you have to do is take the first step and accept that as a reality, a choice, and walk forward, turning this page to uncover more.

** *Start Accepting Now* **

Get ready for more, because that is what I am going to give you over the remainder of this book.

I have my coaching hat on, ready to be your lead support and I am going to tell you exactly what to do.

All you have to do is email me right now at TheMindsetMasterCoach@gmail.com. You will get immediate access to a special gift I have prepared for everyone who decides it is time for change.

A 4-part video series that will start you on your way through the journey of acceptance, awareness, accountability and adaptation. These pages were filled with stories and concept but the videos are all about implementation.

Do yourself the favor you have been wanting to for many years... Start now!

The Dance of Awareness

There were days that awareness was my absolute nightmare; of this I kid you not.

Unearthing the realities of my own creation and the experiences that I drove energy toward was not a fun task in the beginning.

It was exhausting to say the least, and painfully eye opening at best, in the first days of awakening to my people pleasing ways.

When you have spent years sheltering yourself unconsciously from your own actions that have led to very real pains and hurts, turning the light on in the room of darkness is blinding.

With the adjustment of passing time, however, the lights dim, the searing pain of shock when you realize that this has been you all along starts to diminish, and it becomes a dance.

Awareness is the panacea.

Defined by Webster, "panacea" is "the solution or remedy to all difficulties or disease."

In order to create change, you have to understand what it is that you want to change.

If we accept that this path can be changed and was built at least in part by ourselves, we then move into become aware of what we need to change in order to grow.

The reactive state of heightened emotion is not the true problem, it is the direct result of thoughts that were thunk and actions that were executed.

That is where the pot of gold lies, and thus we have to start traversing the path to become aware of those two critical things.

You have traveled parts of my journey with me as I unfolded it into these pages for you to digest, and now it is your turn to switch that light bulb on and illuminate your path to stopping the patterns that cause you to self-destruct.

If you are reading this and are on the path to becoming a recovered people pleaser, I suspect that you have already found some awareness to this character that seemingly runs your life.

The road cannot end here, however.

Awareness is a never-ending march toward a destination that simply moves further and further away. Not because the destination is unattainable but because, as you turn on the awareness in your life, you will start to realize that there is always more, bigger, better, happier that you can achieve.

As I close in on a decade past the first traces of awareness that I had as a people pleaser, I can sincerely concede that awareness should never stop.

The big layers of the people pleaser in me were peeled off quickly and abrasively because they were the most notable, but over time, as my sprint turned to a steady pace, the nuances started to pop up and stripping them away led to even greater freedoms.

As a matter of practice, each day I spend in conscious awareness and reflection of my thoughts, feelings, behaviors, and physical symptoms.

Doing this allows me to ensure that my Patty the People Pleaser doesn't get the chance to cast her vote on my life anymore.

Awareness is your panacea.

It will deliver you from the grip of these veiled attempts of kindness that are creating the illusion of happiness but really are waiting to consume your emotions in anger and resentment.

Before you turn to the next chapter, close this book and pick up a pen. Somewhere that you will remember to go back to, I want you to write down the following:

Today is the day I become aware.

Take the time to invest in the purchase of a pretty journal to chart your path in and start doing it tomorrow.

Every day, commit to entering in your thoughts, feelings, behaviors, and physical symptoms as relates to that people pleaser persona.

Through awareness we find freedom.

*** Start Becoming Aware Now ***

This is your reminder that you have more available to you at your fingertips.

Email me now at:

TheMindsetMasterCoach@gmail.com to get immediate access to your free video series that will guide you down the process of becoming more aware.

"Awareness Is The Greatest

Agent For Change"

~ *Eckhart Tolle*

www.TheIconicMom.com

Go to The Iconic Mom and get access to more information, resources, tools and free downloads today.

Start Living The Way You Would Tell Your Kids To...

The Accountability Checkmate

The day I truly released myself from the stranglehold of Patty was the day that I offered apologies to all those who had gotten caught on the merry-go-round with her.

Each pillar of change is essential. They all hold a unique position in your transformation, but I can truly say that accountability is where most people pleasers get stuck.

Moreover, without accountability you will remain in that place of bitter resentment and frustration forever.

There lies no barrier between you and taking accountability in any situation that you have been in or are in.

Sure, as a child you can't take accountability for the actions of the world around you. An abusive parent, and extreme situation that might have triggered your people pleasing tendencies out of sheer protection, can't be your responsibility.

That said, fast forward however many years it has been as you are reading this book: accountability can be taken now.

If there is one thing that I hope that you gain from this book, is that you have choice.

The experiences that might have happened to you forging your path may have not been on your shoulders, but now, sitting here in present day, you have a choice to continue to allow them to dictate your future or to travel the journey of the pillars of change and be accountable to yourself.

Every day you wake up, you get to make a choice.

Is it going to be a good day or bad day?

Are you going to put yourself first or take care of the world?

Are you going to sit in further resentment and anger because he did this or she said that?

All of that is choice, and accountability will be yours when you have truly accepted that you have a choice and become aware of the destructive tendencies in your life.

In the plethora of abusive relationships I have found myself in over the years of my life, I spent a great deal of time blaming the other person.

Victimized by the way I was being treated.

Saddened that someone could do such things to me.

Miserable that I was handicapped and unable to create change in those people.

That sob story ended the day I took accountability.

I consider myself an intelligent woman and came to realized that I knew better.

In the most simplistic, uncomplicated terms ever.

I knew I didn't feel good on the inside every time I people pleased.

I knew I didn't want to cave to do the things I did.

And yet even though at times I was happy to sit in my delusion, I still knew that it wasn't right.

That was when accountability was a choice I made.

Once I had awareness, I realized that I had co-created every single situation that I had people pleased in as I got older, and that if the experience wasn't in my control, I was still co-creating the energy that I remained focused on it.

Right now you are inspired reading this, and I know it.

You sense freedom on the other pages of this book and you can feel that your life is lingering on the hinge that is accountability.

You are right.

This will change your world forever if you let it.

Where do you start?

You pull it inward.

Pay attention to your language and your thoughts. How often do you find yourself in patterns of blame and projection on to another person?

"I can't believe he didn't even say thank you!"

"Why do I bother even doing it in the first place?"

"No one ever sees how much I put up with and cope with."

Get off the blame train today. Raise your hand in the air, shout a little "toot toot," and stop this train forever.

This is not to say that it's unrealistic to have expectations of others; no one should be treated unfairly. But ask yourself first, are you allowing it?

When I took accountability, I quite literally apologized to the people with whom I co-created worlds of suffering.

This was not me excusing people's behaviors and treatment towards me; this was a way of me claiming control of my life back.

The realization that, in every situation, the pen will always sit in my hand to write the story.

My pen is braced firmly in hand and my story continues to be written the way I choose it to. It is my hope and faith that, after this book, you will pick yours up and start creating the life story you truly want to choose for yourself, not the one you victimized yourself into.

** Start Taking Accountability Now **

This is your reminder that you have more available to you at your fingertips.

Email me now at:

TheMindsetMasterCoach@gmail.com to get immediate access to your free video series that will guide you down the process of becoming more aware.

"Accountability Turns Pain

Into Peace"

~ Anonymous

www.TheIconicMom.com

Go to The Iconic Mom and get access to more information, resources, tools and free downloads today.

Start Living The Way You Would Tell Your Kids To...

The Process of Adaptation

It is common in our society that, when we want to create change, we immediately start to evoke habit and behavioral changes first.

Apologies for the repeat metaphor but, yes, it is the equivalent of putting a Band-Aid over a gunshot wound and expecting the bleeding to stop.

Adaptation has its place, because of course habit and behaviors and actual interruption of those has to occur. However, if you recall the "up to six seconds" rule of subconscious thought, you now realize that the habit is the last piece of the puzzle and thus the reason it is the last of the four pillars of change.

Believe it or not, most adaptation is rather passive and occurs naturally as a result of the first three of the pillars.

Our actions merely start to line up with the thoughts that we have.

Once you realize the degree to which you are a people pleaser and have awareness to how it presents itself in your world, you will find your actions starting to line up with those new thoughts.

That is the reason the first three pillars are the imperative starting points.

In truth, because adaptation happens rather passively, I would much rather spend the greater part of this chapter cautioning you on a common pattern that emerges as we adapt and try to change our world from people pleaser to pleasing ourselves.

If you have at this point decided to commit yourself to removing the shackles of this life, I encourage you to brace yourself, because you are about to shake your world up.

Not just for yourself but for others around you, and at times you may find yourself wanting to crawl back to the comforts of being a "yes woman."

I will state this now bluntly: don't do it!

Keep walking the other side of this people pleasing world. It is truly, well, pleasing!

There are two phenomena that happen when we start to adapt our world and create change and, for the purpose of giving them the attention they deserve, I have dedicated the next two chapters to painting their mural for you.

The Social Closet Renovation

If, like me, you have been a people pleaser all your life, I suspect that your social world is filled with people who you spend your time serving, putting first, and essentially giving all of yourself to when they want it and how they want it.

Ponder that for a minute and consider how much truth there is to that statement.

How many people in your social circle actually serve you, give to you, and elevate you?

Are you the one who always makes the initial point of contact?

If you don't call for days, do you get lambasted because they haven't heard from you?

Do you have many people you can turn to when you need help; do you have *any*?

Husbands, friends, sisters, parents, colleagues -- people pleasers tend to spread their wings over all the spans of their life.

Where does that leave you now that you are stepping into the winds of change?

That leaves you with a lot of people who are conditioned to you being exactly what they want when they want it.

Relationships have been built on a personality trait of yours that has shaped and moulded the expectations of said communion.

And then you change.

You decide you want more, need more, and are putting your foot down on always putting others before yourself.

The results are usually one of two things.

People see your value and watch your happiness and want to ascend with you up the ladder of life. Those relationships deepen.

Or.

People are off put, disturbed, and angry that you are no longer what they need when they want it. Of course a reflection of their own lack of desire, perhaps, to change, but also a condition of the relationship terms that you have all created.

People in your life will fall off and distance themselves from you.

My simple words of insight on this are: accept it.

Be compassionate in understanding that they too have parts of their lives that are unsettled like Patty has unsettled you.

Be accountable and know that, while you are not solely at play in this dynamic, you did co-create it; and thus you'll want to avoid lashing out or enabling further.

Most importantly, remain in a state of self-love. On the journey to understanding how people pleasing has played a role in your life, you will realized that you stopped loving yourself somewhere along the way.

Now is not the time to stop practicing the art of self-love, it is the time to invoke it as law.

Choose relationships that elevate you and who you are becoming.

Choose relationships that are understanding and authentic.

Choose relationships that will allow you to be the authentic version of yourself and not the people pleaser of the past.

Hold all these words in mind as you stare aimlessly at the social closet in front of you and choose wisely, because it is your life you are crafting not just a pair of shoes you are selecting.

The Pendulum Swing

I have always referred to this part of the journey as the pendulum swing but, as I wrote it out just now, I actually visualized it far more as a pendulum that is toting a wrecking ball on the end of the chain.

You are about to open your eyes wide, taking in all the information that you have gained from this book and likely feeling all the emotions that go along with it.

You are going to see people pleasing in everything you do.

You are going to get confused about when you are people pleasing and when you are actually wanting to help others in genuine care.

You are going to swing the pendulum hard and fast because, now that you are awakened to all of this, you want to have it changed yesterday.

I, however, encourage you to be wary of swinging the pendulum too fast and furiously.

In the path of that pendulum are a lot of people and ones who you truly do care about.

People who, through no fault of their own, have been cast into the world with you as a people pleaser.

In some cases, perhaps it has been decades that you have been this way. Perhaps the anguish of people pleasing has been felt and experienced in isolation so your loved ones don't even have knowledge of your pain.

You are going to want to say "no" to everything, refuse to run mindless errands and be more independent in your day-to-day life.

If the pendulum swings too mightily, it will plow people over along the way and lead to a great deal of confusion. Of course, these are waters that you can navigate, but why sail rough seas when you can be on open ocean that is calm.

I experienced this myself and it shook the foundations for a period of time in my relationships, where people almost didn't recognize me because I stepped too far over into the world of not people pleasing.

Inevitably I settled in the middle and found my course, and you will too.

Facilitate your journey by bringing people into the light with you. Keeping them in the dark will only cause more alarm when the pendulum strikes them on the way by.

Explain your story and let them into the journey with you so instead of being alone you can sail the uncharted waters together.

Tomorrow is a New Day

Five words are sitting directly above this line that you are reading right now. Five words that, as I typed them, my emotions settled into an unexpected place.

Literally sitting on the verge of tears as I craft these final words to you, the instrumental music humming in my ears that is taking on an inspiring tone isn't helping my eyes stay water free.

Between the covers of this book are words written that very few people even know the stories to. Words that have been mine to experience and to grow from.

The shame and embarrassment of my journey to being a recovered people pleaser have been long gone, and yet as I type this, I can't help but feel a cathartic release of days gone by.

A surge of feelings as I reflect back in rapid-fire fashion on the stories that I have shared.

Stories selected from a slew of possibilities that could have been drawn upon to help you see the light in front of you on your path.

Stories that I cried through as I typed them to you, smiled at and chuckled when I realized how ridiculous they sounded in my ears, and relinquished from my reality a long time ago.

The scars, both literal and figurative, have long since faded to distant memories, but I sit in complete gratitude that the visceral emotion of my past hasn't ever left me.

I choose not to forget from where I have come because, if I do, I lose the contact point of how I can serve you, elevate you, and empathize wholly with you.

Your pain is my pain.

Your hurts are mine as well.

Your struggles, while different in context, are similar in driver.

I understand you because I was you.

I have poured the darkest stories of my life out to you here not to seek sympathy for what I have experienced but to reach out my hand and offer it to you so we can walk together.

To inspire you to know that what you might be living doesn't have to be.

To inform you to know how to start creating change now, without need for more.

I am blessed every day to coach and mentor women and moms around the world and help them carve a new path, free from this people pleasing grip, and yet I am always looking for more.

More ways to share.

More ways to inspire.

More ways to reach...

You.

Her.

They.

Us.

The world in which we live as people pleasers can often feel isolated and dark, void of any true genuine care of others.

It doesn't have to be that way.

Patterns can be broken. Habits changed and thoughts created in a new day, new life, and new you.

The you that is authentic to yourself.

The you that is continually ascending and reaching new levels in life.

The you that, at the core, really is just a loving soul who wants to heal the world, spread light and love, and lift people up.

Stand in the mirror right now; pretend I am standing beside you with hand in yours so that you can feel you are not alone.

Your words might fall short to yourself, and your mind likely won't believe you.

So don't worry, let me do the talking:

"You are not alone.

"Let me take your hand and walk with you.

"Let me walk with you, my friend, because I have traveled the road you are navigating and I know my way.

"Together we will find yours."

My Job Here With You Is Not Done...

As you have read through the pages of this book the likelihood that emotion has stirred in you is high.

Perhaps your soul has been stirred and you have unearthed a side of yourself that you wish to release from.

Or you have come into greater realization of the chains that are keeping you locked away from true freedom.

You read these words and you felt with me, traveled a journey with me and perhaps even cried with me.

And while reading this book may have offered you a fragment of clarity and lit the path in front of you to start walking I want to serve you better.

My purpose and the reason I created The Iconic Mom and am a Master Mindset Coach is to breathe life into your world and offer you freedom from what is holding you back.

You deserve more.

You want more.

Let's together create more.

And so that is why I am not stopping here, I have more for you.

While I can't sit beside you and force you to take this step towards freedom I can tell you that if you decide to do this you will position yourself to create life changing experiences.

Go to www.TheIconicMom.com/soulcall and fill out the form to get your free Soul Call today. Once you fill out the form I will personally connect with you to schedule our private call.

Don't waste another second staying locked when there's a whole life to start creating.

Start living your life the way you would tell your kids to.

Love Shaking You Up!

Carrie Campbell

The Mindset Master Coach and Mom Mentor

www.TheIconicMom.com

About The Author

Carrie Campbell is a Licensed Counselor and Mindset Master Coach with fifteen years' experience working in clinical settings. Her clients have ranged from competitive athletes and high-end business folk to alcoholics and children with special needs.

Also a professional model.

Powerlifter and physique athlete.

Mom.

And wife.

But those are just her "labels'.

'Who' she is has nothing to do with any of that.

Because to the core she is love.

She is hope, she is faith and she is unlimited.

To uncover her true essence, she traveled a journey that saw her take the oftentimes challenging steps of bringing brightness to her shadows.

Light to my darkness.

She was once in a hole. And she found her way out.

Let her jump in the hole with you...

...And show you the way.

23694819R00084

Made in the USA
San Bernardino, CA
29 January 2019